W9-AAZ-733

world
tapas

THE AUSTRALIAN
Women's Weekly

CONTENTS

AUSTRALIAN CUP AND
SPOON MEASUREMENTS
ARE METRIC.
A CONVERSION CHART
APPEARS ON PAGE 77.

We've compiled our favourite Spanish tapas,
Greek mezze and Italian antipasto recipes
into this little book. These flavoursome
dishes are perfect for sharing among friends.
Choose one to serve with a pre-dinner drink,
or prepare a selection for a delicious and
dynamic meal.

Pamela Clark

Food Director

MINI CHICKEN SOUVLAKIA

prep & cook time 35 minutes (+ refrigeration) makes 20
nutritional count per skewer 5.4g total fat
(1.4g saturated fat); 364kJ (87 cal);
0.1g carbohydrate; 9.4g protein; 0.1g fibre

1kg (2 pounds) chicken thigh fillets
2 tablespoons olive oil
2 tablespoons lemon juice
⅓ cup finely chopped fresh mint
2 cloves garlic, crushed
1½ teaspoons smoked paprika

1 Trim any fat from chicken; cut chicken into
2cm (1 inch) thick strips. Combine chicken in
medium bowl with remaining ingredients.
Thread chicken onto 20 bamboo skewers;
cover, refrigerate 3 hours or overnight.
2 Cook skewers on heated oiled grill plate (or
grill or barbecue) until browned and cooked
through. Serve with lemon wedges, if you like.
notes Soak the skewers in cold water for at least
30 minutes before using to prevent them scorching
during cooking.
For optimum flavour, marinate the chicken overnight.

deep-fried whitebait

DEEP-FRIED WHITEBAIT

prep & cook time **45 minutes** serves **4**
nutritional count per serving **35.4g total fat**
(9.9g saturated fat); 2337kJ (559 cal);
30.4g carbohydrate; 29.3g protein; 1.9g fibre

1 cup (150g) plain (all-purpose) flour
¼ cup coarsely chopped fresh
   coriander (cilantro)
500g (1 pound) whitebait
vegetable oil, for deep-frying
cucumber garlic dip
20g (¾ ounce) ghee
½ teaspoon each ground coriander
   and ground cumin
¾ cup (210g) yogurt
1 lebanese cucumber (130g), seeded,
   chopped finely
1 clove garlic, crushed
1 tablespoon lemon juice

1 Make cucumber garlic dip
2 Combine flour and fresh coriander in
large bowl; add whitebait, in batches, toss
until coated.
3 Heat oil in medium saucepan; deep-fry
whitebait, in batches, until browned and
cooked through. Drain on absorbent paper.
Serve with spiced yogurt dip.
cucumber garlic dip Heat ghee in small
saucepan; cook ground spices, stirring, until
fragrant, cool. Combine yogurt, cucumber,
garlic and juice in small bowl for dip; stir in
spice mixture.

garlic and paprika char-grilled prawns

GARLIC AND PAPRIKA CHAR-GRILLED PRAWNS

prep & cook time **30 minutes** serves **6**
nutritional count per serving **12.5g total fat**
(1.8g saturated fat); 652kJ (156 cal);
1.2g carbohydrate; 9.7g protein; 0.5g fibre

12 uncooked medium king prawns
   (shrimp) (540g)
1 medium red capsicum (bell pepper)
   (200g), chopped coarsely
⅓ cup (80ml) olive oil
2 cloves garlic, crushed
1 teaspoon smoked paprika

1 Shell and devein prawns, leaving tails intact.
2 Combine prawns, capsicum, oil, garlic and
paprika in medium bowl.
3 Cook capsicum on heated grill plate (or grill
or barbecue) until browned both sides. Add
prawns towards the end of capsicum cooking
time; cook, turning, until prawns are changed
in colour.
4 Serve with lemon wedges, if you like.

pan-seared scallops with anchovy butter

PAN-SEARED SCALLOPS WITH ANCHOVY BUTTER

prep & cook time **15 minutes** serves **4**
nutritional count per serving **9.1g total fat**
(4.8g saturated fat); 514kJ (123 cal);
0.8g carbohydrate; 9.6g protein; 0.3g fibre

2 teaspoons olive oil
12 scallops (300g), roe removed
30g (1 ounce) butter
3 drained anchovy fillets
2 cloves garlic, crushed
2 teaspoons lemon juice
1 tablespoon finely chopped fresh chives

1 Heat oil in large frying pan; cook scallops, both sides, until browned lightly. Remove from pan; cover to keep warm.
2 Add butter, anchovies and garlic to pan; cook, stirring, until garlic is browned lightly. Return scallops to pan with juice; cook until scallops are heated through. Serve scallops drizzled with anchovy butter and sprinkled with chives.

COD AND OLIVE FRITTERS

prep & cook time **1 hour 30 minutes** (+ refrigeration)
makes **40** nutritional count per fritter **2.6g total fat**
(0.4g saturated fat); 196kJ (47 cal);
47.4g carbohydrate; 3.6g protein; 0.3g fibre

650g (1¼ pounds) salted cod fillet, skin on
3 medium potatoes (600g), halved
1 tablespoon olive oil
1 medium brown onion (150g),
    chopped finely
2 cloves garlic, crushed
¼ cup finely chopped fresh flat-leaf parsley
½ cup (60g) seeded green olives,
    chopped finely
1 egg
vegetable oil, for deep-frying

1 Rinse fish under cold water to remove excess salt. Place fish in large bowl, cover with cold water; refrigerate, covered, overnight, changing the water three or four times. Drain fish; discard water.
2 Place fish in large saucepan, cover with cold water; bring to the boil uncovered. Reduce heat, simmer, covered, 5 minutes. Drain fish, discard water; remove skin and bones then flake fish.
3 Boil, steam or microwave potato until tender; drain. Roughly mash potato in large bowl.
4 Meanwhile, heat olive oil in large frying pan; cook onion and garlic, stirring, until onion softens.
5 Combine fish, onion mixture, parsley, olives and egg with potato; mix well.
6 Roll level tablespoons of fish mixture into balls, place on baking-paper (parchment) lined tray; refrigerate 30 minutes.
7 Heat vegetable oil in deep medium saucepan; deep-fry fritters, in batches, until browned lightly and heated through. Drain on absorbent paper.

note Salted cod, also known as salt cod, baccalà, bacalhau, bacalao and morue, is available from Italian, Spanish and Portuguese delicatessens and some speciality food stores. It needs to be de-salted and rehydrated before use.

cod and olive fritters

warm citrus seafood salad

WARM CITRUS SEAFOOD SALAD

prep & cook time **1 hour 15 minutes (+ refrigeration)**
serves **6** nutritional count per serving **28.7g total fat**
(4.1g saturated fat); 1630kJ (390 cal);
1.5g carbohydrate; 32.1g protein; 0.1g fibre

500g (1 pound) baby octopus
250g (8 ounces) small calamari hoods
1kg (2 pounds) medium uncooked
**   prawns (shrimp)**
1 tablespoon each coarsely chopped
**   fresh flat-leaf parsley and fresh mint**
citrus dressing
⅓ cup (80ml) lemon juice
¾ cup (180ml) olive oil
1 teaspoon finely grated orange rind
1 teaspoon white sugar
1 clove garlic, crushed

1 Make citrus dressing.
2 Remove and discard heads and beaks from octopus. Cut calamari lengthways down centre; lay out flat with inside facing upwards. Make shallow cuts diagonally across calamari; cut into 2cm (1 inch) slices in opposite direction. Shell and devein prawns, leaving tails intact.
3 Combine all seafood with half of the citrus dressing in large bowl, cover; refrigerate 3 hours or overnight.
4 Drain seafood, discard marinade. Cook seafood, in batches, on heated oiled grill plate (or grill or barbecue) until browned lightly and just changed in colour. Toss warm seafood with remaining citrus dressing and herbs.
citrus dressing Combine ingredients in screw-top jar; shake well.

char-grilled chilli octopus

CHAR-GRILLED CHILLI OCTOPUS

prep & cook time **1 hour (+ refrigeration)** serves **6**
nutritional count per serving **11g total fat**
(1.7g saturated fat); 857kJ (205 cal);
1.7g carbohydrate; 24.8g protein; 0.5g fibre

1kg (2 pounds) baby octopus
¼ cup (60ml) olive oil
⅓ cup (80ml) lemon juice
6 cloves garlic, crushed
2 fresh small red thai (serrano) chillies,
**   chopped finely**
1 tablespoon sweet paprika

1 Remove and discard heads and beaks from octopus; cut each octopus in half. Combine octopus with remaining ingredients in medium bowl, cover; refrigerate 3 hours or overnight.
2 Cook octopus, in batches, on heated oiled grill plate (or grill or barbecue) until tender.

CARAMELISED TOMATO AND HAM BITES

prep & cook time **40 minutes** makes **16**
nutritional count per bite **7.5g total fat**
(4.1g saturated fat); 644kJ (154 cal);
12.7g carbohydrate; 8.4g protein; 0.7g fibre

Cook 2 finely chopped shallots in heated oiled medium frying pan until soft. Add 250g (8 ounces) halved cherry tomatoes; cook 5 minutes. Add ¼ cup balsamic vinegar and 1 tablespoon brown sugar; cook, stirring occasionally, until thickened. Cut 1 brioche loaf into 16 slices; cut 32 x 6.5cm (2½ inch) rounds from slices. Top half the slices with 2 cups finely grated semi-hard sheep-milk cheese; grill until cheese melts. Toast remaining rounds until golden. Divide 185g (6 ounces) thinly sliced double smoked leg ham among toast rounds; top each with caramelised tomatoes, top with remaining toasts. Serve warm.

PRAWN AND CAPER SANDWICHES

prep time **30 minutes** makes **36**
nutritional count per triangle **2.6g total fat**
(0.3g saturated fat); 255kJ (61 cal);
7g carbohydrate; 2.1g protein; 0.4g fibre

Combine 300g (9½ ounces) cooked, shelled, finely chopped prawns (shrimp), ¼ cup rinsed drained, finely chopped capers, 1 teaspoon sweet paprika, 1 cup mayonnaise, ¼ cup finely chopped fresh flat-leaf parsley and 1 crushed garlic clove in medium bowl. Divide prawn mixture between 9 slices of white bread; top with another 9 slices bread. Trim crusts; cut each sandwich into four triangles.

BITES

ASPARAGUS AND COPPA SALAD BITES

prep time **15 minutes** makes **10**
nutritional count per bite **11.4g total fat**
(4.6g saturated fat); 744kJ (178 cal);
11.5g carbohydrate; 6.9g protein; 1.1g fibre

Boil, steam or microwave 170g (5½ ounces) trimmed asparagus; drain. Finely chop asparagus; combine with 1 finely chopped small red onion, 2 tablespoons finely chopped fresh basil, 2 teaspoons red wine vinegar and 2 tablespoons olive oil in medium bowl. Split 10 mini croissants in half. Divide 200g (6½ ounces) thinly sliced coppa among half the croissants; top with asparagus mixture, then remaining croissant halves. Serve at room temperature.

BLUE CHEESE AND FIG BITES

prep & cook time **20 minutes** makes **12**
nutritional count per bite **11.9g total fat**
(2.9g saturated fat); 1012kJ (242 cal);
25.5g carbohydrate; 6.2g protein; 3.9g fibre

Process ⅓ cup roasted slivered almonds with 2 coarsely chopped green onions (scallions), 1 cup loosely packed fresh mint leaves, ⅓ cup olive oil and 1 tablespoon lemon juice until smooth. Halve 1 long turkish loaf lengthways; cut each half lengthways into 3 fingers then cut fingers into four crossways to get 24 slices. Toast bread under hot grill (broiler). Spread almond mixture on half the toasts; top with 200g (6½ ounces) thinly sliced semi-dried figs and 100g (3 ounces) thinly sliced blue cheese. Top with remaining toast; serve warm.

broad beans and thyme

ARTICHOKE AND ASPARAGUS FRITTERS WITH OLIVE RELISH

prep & cook time **40 minutes**   makes **15**
nutritional count per fritter **4.6g total fat**
(1.2g saturated fat); 288kJ (69 cal);
3.8g carbohydrate; 2.9g protein; 0.8g fibre

170g (5½ ounces) asparagus, trimmed,
   chopped finely
280g (9 ounces) bottled artichokes in brine,
   drained, chopped finely
2 eggs
2 tablespoons finely chopped fresh mint
½ cup (40g) finely grated parmesan cheese
¼ cup (35g) self-raising flour
vegetable oil, for shallow frying
olive relish
½ cup (60g) each seeded green olives and
   seeded black olives, chopped finely
¼ cup finely chopped fresh flat-leaf parsley
1 tablespoon finely chopped fresh chives
1 tablespoon olive oil
1 tablespoon lemon juice

1 Make olive relish.
2 Combine asparagus, artichoke, eggs, mint,
cheese and flour in medium bowl.
3 Heat oil in large frying pan; shallow-fry
heaped tablespoons of fritter mixture, in
batches, until browned all over and cooked
through. Drain fritters on absorbent paper;
serve hot with olive relish.
olive relish Combine ingredients in small bowl.

BROAD BEANS AND THYME

prep & cook time **40 minutes**   serves **4**
nutritional count per serving **7.7g total fat**
(3.5g saturated fat); 589kJ (141 cal);
2g carbohydrate; 13.9g protein; 4.8g fibre

600g (1¼ pounds) frozen broad beans
   (fava beans), thawed
10g (½ ounce) butter
2 shallots (50g), chopped finely
150g (4½ ounces) speck, chopped finely
1 tablespoon fresh thyme leaves
1 tablespoon lemon juice

1 Drop beans into medium saucepan of
boiling water, return to the boil; drain. When
beans are cool enough to handle, peel away
grey-coloured outer shells.
2 Heat butter in large frying pan; cook shallot
and speck, stirring, until speck is browned
lightly. Add beans and thyme; cook, stirring,
until beans are heated through. Stir in juice.

artichoke and asparagus fritters with olive relish

soft-shell crabs with green onion aioli

SOFT-SHELL CRABS WITH GREEN ONION AÏOLI

prep & cook time **30 minutes** serves **8**
nutritional count per serving **13g total fat**
(1.5g saturated fat); 920kJ (220 cal);
16.7g carbohydrate; 9g protein; 0.6g fibre

½ cup (100g) rice flour
1 teaspoon dried chilli flakes
2 teaspoons sea salt
8 uncooked small soft-shell crabs (500g)
vegetable oil, for deep frying
1 cup loosely packed fresh basil leaves
green onion aïoli
¾ cup (225g) mayonnaise
2 green onions (scallions), sliced finely
1 clove garlic, crushed
1 tablespoon lemon juice

1 Make green onion aïoli.
2 Combine flour, chilli and salt in medium bowl.
3 Clean crabs; pat dry then cut into quarters. Coat crab quarters with flour mixture; shake away excess.
4 Heat oil in large saucepan; deep-fry basil about 30 seconds or until crisp. Drain on absorbent paper. Deep-fry crabs, in batches, until browned lightly. Drain on absorbent paper. Serve with basil and aïoli.
green onion aïoli Combine ingredients in small bowl.

grilled mussels with prosciutto

GRILLED MUSSELS WITH PROSCIUTTO

prep & cook time **30 minutes** serves **4**
nutritional count per serving **17.6g total fat**
(11.2g saturated fat); 773kJ (185 cal);
1.8g carbohydrate; 5.5g protein; 0.2g fibre

20 small black mussels (500g)
2 cups (500ml) water
80g (2½ ounces) butter, softened
50g (1½ ounces) thinly sliced prosciutto, chopped finely
1 clove garlic, crushed
2 green onions (scallions), chopped finely

1 Scrub mussels; remove beards. Bring the water to the boil in large saucepan. Add the mussels, cover; boil about 3 minutes or until mussels open (discard any that do not).
2 Drain mussels; discard liquid. Break open shells; discard top shell. Loosen mussels from shells with a spoon; return mussels to shells, place in single layer on oven tray.
3 Preheat grill (broiler).
4 Combine butter, prosciutto, garlic and onion in small bowl. Divide butter mixture over mussels; grill about 3 minutes or until browned lightly.

rosemary potatoes with leek and chorizo

ROSEMARY POTATOES WITH LEEK AND CHORIZO

prep & cook time **45 minutes** serves **8**
nutritional count per serving **19.8g total fat**
(5.6g saturated fat); 1120kJ (268 cal);
11g carbohydrate; 10.6g protein; 2.9g fibre

500g (1 pound) baby new potatoes,
   sliced thickly
2 chorizo sausages (340g), cut into
   1cm (½ inch) thick slices
1 large leek (500g), trimmed, chopped coarsely
6 cloves garlic
1 tablespoon finely chopped fresh rosemary
2 teaspoons sweet paprika
5 bay leaves
¼ cup (60ml) olive oil

1 Preheat oven to 200°C/400°F.
2 Combine ingredients in large baking dish.
Roast, uncovered, about 30 minutes or until
potatoes are browned lightly.

ROASTED THYME POTATOES WITH SPICY SAUCE

prep & cook time **45 minutes** serves **8**
nutritional count per serving **7g total fat**
(1g saturated fat); 506kJ (121 cal);
11.5g carbohydrate; 2.1g protein; 2.2g fibre

500g (1 pound) baby new potatoes, halved
2 tablespoons olive oil
1 tablespoon finely chopped fresh thyme
spicy sauce
1 tablespoon olive oil
1 small brown onion (80g), chopped finely
2 cloves garlic, sliced thinly
1 fresh small red thai (serrano) chilli,
   chopped finely
410g (13 ounces) canned crushed tomatoes
2 teaspoons caster (superfine) sugar

1 Preheat oven to 200°C/400°F.
2 Combine potatoes, oil and thyme in large
baking dish; roast about 30 minutes or until
potato is tender.
3 Meanwhile, make spicy sauce.
4 Serve spicy sauce with hot roasted potatoes.
spicy sauce Heat oil in medium saucepan;
cook onion, garlic and chilli, stirring occasionally,
until onion is soft. Add undrained tomatoes
and sugar; bring to the boil. Reduce heat;
simmer, uncovered, stirring occasionally, about
10 minutes or until sauce thickens.

roasted thyme potatoes with spicy sauce

veal meatballs with gazpacho salsa

VEAL MEATBALLS WITH GAZPACHO SALSA

prep & cook time **50 minutes** makes **40**
nutritional count per meatball **4.1g total fat**
(1.1g saturated fat); 247kJ (59 cal);
1.7g carbohydrate; 3.7g protein; 0.3g fibre

1 tablespoon olive oil
1 large brown onion (200g), chopped finely
2 cloves garlic, crushed
500g (1 pound) minced (ground) veal
2 tablespoons finely chopped fresh oregano
1½ cups (120g) finely grated
    manchego cheese
1 cup (70g) stale breadcrumbs
1 egg
vegetable oil, for shallow-frying
gazpacho salsa
1 lebanese cucumber (130g), seeded,
    chopped finely
1 medium green capsicum (bell pepper)
    (200g), chopped finely
½ small red onion (50g), chopped finely
1 small tomato (30g), seeded, chopped finely
2 tablespoons olive oil
1 tablespoon sherry vinegar

1 Make gazpacho salsa.
2 Heat olive oil in medium frying pan; cook onion and garlic, stirring, until onion softens. Cool 5 minutes.
3 Combine onion mixture, veal, oregano, cheese, breadcrumbs and egg in large bowl. Roll rounded tablespoons of the veal mixture into balls.
4 Heat vegetable oil in large frying pan; shallow-fry meatballs, in batches, until cooked through. Drain on absorbent paper. Serve hot with gazpacho salsa.
gazpacho salsa Combine ingredients in small bowl.

anchovy and goat's cheese baked mushrooms

ANCHOVY AND GOAT'S CHEESE BAKED MUSHROOMS

prep & cook time **40 minutes** makes **20**
nutritional count per mushroom **4.1g total fat**
(1.1g saturated fat); 276kJ (66 cal);
4.3g carbohydrate; 2.7g protein; 0.8g fibre

20 large button mushrooms (400g)
1¾ cups (120g) stale breadcrumbs
120g (4 ounces) soft goat's cheese
¼ cup (60ml) olive oil
4 drained anchovy fillets, chopped finely
⅓ cup finely chopped fresh chives
1 cup (250ml) chicken stock

1 Preheat oven to 200°C/400°F.
2 Remove and discard stems from mushrooms; place mushroom caps, in single layer, in medium baking dish.
3 Combine breadcrumbs, cheese, oil, anchovy and chives in medium bowl. Stuff mushrooms with mixture.
4 Add stock to baking dish; bake, uncovered, about 15 minutes or until mushrooms are browned lightly.

ROASTED VEGETABLE AND MASCARPONE TERRINE

prep & cook time **1 hour 30 minutes (+ refrigeration)**
makes **16 slices** nutritional count per slice **14.9g total fat**
(9.4g saturated fat); 702kJ (168 cal);
1.9g carbohydrate; 6.7g protein; 0.7g fibre

1 medium red capsicum (bell pepper) (200g)
1 medium zucchini (120g), sliced
thinly lengthways
2 baby eggplants (120g), sliced
thinly lengthways
12 slices prosciutto (180g)
250g (8 ounces) mascarpone cheese
2 eggs
¼ cup finely chopped fresh basil

1 Preheat oven to 200°C/400°F.
2 Quarter capsicums; discard seeds and membranes. Roast, skin-side up, until skin blisters and blackens. Cover capsicum with plastic or paper for 5 minutes; peel away skin, then chop capsicum finely.
3 Meanwhile, cook zucchini and eggplant, in batches, on heated oiled grill plate (or grill or barbecue) until tender; cool. Chop vegetables finely.
4 Reduce oven temperature to 180°C/350°F. Oil 8cm x 26cm (3 inch x 10 inch) bar pan.
5 Line base and sides of pan with prosciutto, leaving 7cm (3 inch) overhang on sides of pan.
6 Combine cheese and eggs in medium bowl; stir in vegetables and basil. Carefully spread mixture into pan; fold prosciutto over to cover mixture. Cover pan tightly with foil; place on oven tray.
7 Roast terrine 30 minutes. Uncover, roast about 30 minutes or until terrine is firm. Cool. Refrigerate terrine 3 hours before cutting into 16 slices.

roasted vegetable and mascarpone terrine

braised artichokes with crunchy almond topping

BRAISED ARTICHOKES WITH CRUNCHY ALMOND TOPPING

prep & cook time **1 hour 40 minutes** serves **6**
nutritional count per serving **13.1g total fat**
(1.9g saturated fat); 928kJ (222 cal);
13.1g carbohydrate; 11.6g protein; 3.3g fibre

6 large globe artichokes (2.4kg)
4 bay leaves
4 cloves garlic
1 litre (4 cups) chicken stock
crunchy almond topping
¾ cup (50g) stale breadcrumbs
⅓ cup (25g) flaked almonds
2 tablespoons finely chopped fresh
    flat-leaf parsley
½ cup (60g) seeded green olives,
    chopped finely
¼ cup (60ml) olive oil
1 tablespoon finely grated lemon rind
2 tablespoons lemon juice

1 Preheat oven to 200°C/400°F.
2 Prepare artichokes by snapping off tough outer leaves and peeling stems. Trim stems to 5cm (2 inches). Cut 2cm (1 inch) off top of artichokes to reveal chokes. Cut artichokes in half from top to bottom, then scoop out and discard furry chokes from the centres. As you finish preparing each artichoke, place it in a large bowl of water containing the juice of about half a lemon (this stops any discolouration while you are preparing the next one).
3 Drain artichokes. Combine artichokes, bay leaves, garlic and stock in small baking dish, ensuring artichokes are covered with stock. Bake, covered, about 45 minutes or until artichokes are tender.
4 Meanwhile, make crunchy almond topping.
5 Drain artichokes; discard liquid.
6 Serve artichokes hot or at room temperature; sprinkle with crunchy almond topping.
crunchy almond topping Combine breadcrumbs and nuts on oven tray; roast about 5 minutes, cool 5 minutes. Combine breadcrumb mixture with remaining ingredients in small bowl.

smoked trout dip

FRIED BOCCONCINI WITH ROASTED CAPSICUM SAUCE

prep & cook time **1 hour** makes **16**
nutritional count per cheese ball **4.5g total fat**
(2.1g saturated fat); 309kJ (74 cal);
3.8g carbohydrate; 4.3g protein; 0.5g fibre

1 medium red capsicum (bell-pepper) (200g)
2 medium egg (plum) tomatoes (150g), halved
2 cloves garlic, unpeeled
2 teaspoons olive oil
2 tablespoons plain (all-purpose) flour
1 egg, beaten lightly
½ cup (50g) packaged breadcrumbs
¼ cup (20g) finely grated parmesan cheese
2 tablespoons finely chopped fresh
    flat-leaf parsley
2 teaspoons finely grated lemon rind
16 cherry bocconcini cheese (240g)
vegetable oil, for deep-frying

1 Preheat oven to 200°C/400°F.
2 Quarter capsicum; remove seeds and membranes. Combine capsicum, tomato, garlic and oil in small baking dish; roast, uncovered, about 20 minutes or until vegetables soften.
3 Peel garlic; blend or process garlic and vegetable mixture until smooth.
4 Place flour and egg in separate small shallow bowls. Combine breadcrumbs, parmesan, parsley and rind in another small shallow bowl.
5 Coat bocconcini in flour; shake off excess. Dip in egg, then in breadcrumb mixture.
6 Meanwhile heat oil in wok; deep-fry bocconcini, in batches, until golden. Drain on wire rack over tray.
7 Serve bocconcini with sauce.

SMOKED TROUT DIP

prep & cook time **30 minutes** makes **1½ cups**
nutritional count per teaspoon **0.7g total fat**
(0.1g saturated fat); 46kJ (11 cal);
0.4g carbohydrate; 0.7g protein; 0.1g fibre

1 medium potato (200g), chopped coarsely
¼ cup (60ml) warm milk
150g (4½ ounce) piece smoked trout, flaked
1 clove garlic, crushed
2 tablespoons olive oil
2 green onions (scallions), chopped finely

1 Boil, steam or microwave potato until tender; drain. Push potato through fine sieve into small bowl; stir in milk.
2 Combine trout, garlic, oil and onion in medium bowl; fold in potato mixture.
3 Serve dip with poppy seed crackers or the garlic pizza wedges on page 33, if you like.

fried bocconcini with roasted capsicum sauce

risotto-filled zucchini flowers

RISOTTO-FILLED ZUCCHINI FLOWERS

prep & cook time 1 hour 30 minutes (+ cooking)
makes 28 nutritional count per flower 1.8g total fat
(1g saturated fat); 209kJ (50 cal);
6.2g carbohydrate; 1.3g protein; 0.4g fibre

2 cups (500ml) chicken stock
½ cup (125ml) dry white wine
pinch saffron
40g (1½ ounces) butter
1 small brown onion (80g), chopped finely
1 clove garlic, crushed
1 cup (200g) arborio rice
⅓ cup (25g) finely grated parmesan cheese
1 teaspoon finely grated lemon rind
2 tablespoons finely chopped fresh
    flat-leaf parsley
28 zucchini flowers with stem attached (420g)
cooking-oil spray

1 Combine stock, wine and saffron in medium saucepan; bring to the boil. Reduce heat; simmer, covered.

2 Meanwhile, melt butter in medium saucepan; cook onion and garlic, stirring, until onion softens. Add rice; stir over medium heat until rice is coated in butter mixture. Stir in ½ cup of the simmering stock mixture; cook, stirring, over low heat until liquid is absorbed. Continue adding stock mixture, in ½-cup batches, stirring, until liquid is absorbed after each addition. Total cooking time should be about 35 minutes or until rice is tender. Stir in cheese, rind and parsley, cover; cool 30 minutes.

3 Preheat oven to 200°C/400°F. Oil two oven trays.

4 Discard stamens from zucchini flowers; fill flowers with 1 level tablespoon of risotto mixture, twist petal tops to enclose filling.

5 Place zucchini flowers on trays; spray all over with cooking-oil spray. Roast, uncovered, about 15 minutes or until zucchini stems are tender.

note The stem of the zucchini is the baby zucchini attached to the flower.

SPINACH AND FETTA TRIANGLES

prep & cook time **1 hour 30 minutes** makes **48**
nutritional count per triangle **4.8g total fat**
(3g saturated fat); 280kJ (67 cal);
3.9g carbohydrate; 1.9g protein; 0.3g fibre

2 teaspoons olive oil
3 green onions (scallions), chopped finely
250g (8 ounces) baby spinach leaves
250g (8 ounces) fetta cheese, crumbled
2 tablespoons finely chopped fresh
   flat-leaf parsley
1 tablespoon finely chopped fresh dill
1 egg
24 sheets fillo pastry
150g (4½ ounces) ghee or butter, melted

1 Heat oil in large frying pan, add onion; cook, stirring, until onion is softened. Add spinach; cook, stirring, until spinach is wilted. Remove from heat. When cool enough to handle, squeeze excess moisture from spinach; chop coarsely.

2 Combine spinach mixture in medium bowl with cheese, herbs and egg.

3 Preheat oven to 200°C/400°F. Oil oven trays; line with baking paper (parchment).

4 Brush 1 sheet of pastry with ghee; top with a second sheet and brush with ghee. Cut layered sheets into 4 strips lengthways. Place rounded teaspoons of spinach mixture at one end of each strip. Fold one corner of pastry diagonally over filling to form a triangle. Continue folding to end of strip, retaining triangular shape. Brush triangles with a little ghee. Repeat to make a total of 48 triangles.

5 Place triangles on trays. Bake 15 minutes or until browned lightly.

spinach and fetta triangles

garlic pizza wedges

GARLIC PIZZA WEDGES

prep & cook time **1 hour (+ standing)** makes **32**
nutritional count per wedge **0.9g total fat**
(0.2g saturated fat); 209kJ (50 cal);
8.6g carbohydrate; 1.5g protein; 0.5g fibre

1 cup (250ml) warm water
1 teaspoon caster (superfine) sugar
7g (¼ ounce) sachet dried yeast
2½ cups (375g) plain (all-purpose) flour
1 teaspoon salt
1 tablespoon olive oil
2 cloves garlic, crushed
2 tablespoons finely grated parmesan cheese

1 Combine the water, sugar and yeast in small jug. Stand in warm place about 10 minutes or until frothy.

2 Sift flour and salt into large bowl. Add yeast mixture; mix to a soft dough. Knead dough on floured surface about 10 minutes or until smooth and elastic. Place dough in oiled large bowl; cover. Stand in warm place about 1 hour or until dough has doubled in size.

3 Preheat oven to 220°C/425°F. Grease two oven or pizza trays.

4 Divide dough in half. Roll each portion into a 30cm (12 inch) round; place on trays.

5 Brush pizza bases with combined oil and garlic; sprinkle with cheese.

6 Bake pizzas about 20 minutes or until browned and crisp. Cut each pizza into 16 wedges.

note **These garlic wedges are great with dips.**

SALMON CARPACCIO

prep time **30 minutes (+ freezing and refrigeration)**
serves **8** nutritional count per serving **5.9g total fat**
(1.1g saturated fat); 414kJ (99 cal);
1.3g carbohydrate; 10g protein; 0.6g fibre

Tightly wrap 400g (12½ ounce) piece sashimi
salmon in plastic wrap; freeze 1 hour. Unwrap
salmon; slice thinly. Arrange salmon on serving
platter; drizzle with 2 tablespoons white wine
vinegar. Refrigerate 1 hour. Slice 2 baby fennel
bulbs thinly. Reserve 2 teaspoons finely
chopped fennel fronds. Combine fennel,
fronds, 2 teaspoons finely grated orange rind,
¼ cup orange juice, 1 tablespoon olive oil
and 1 teaspoon finely chopped fresh thyme
in medium bowl. Drain excess vinegar from
salmon; serve topped with fennel mixture.

ZUCCHINI CARPACCIO

prep time **20 minutes (+ refrigeration)** serves **8**
nutritional count per serving **6g total fat**
(0.7g saturated fat); 464kJ (111 cal);
12.5g carbohydrate; 1.3g protein; 1.3g fibre

Using vegetable peeler, slice 3 large zucchinis
lengthways into ribbons. Combine zucchini in
medium bowl with 2 tablespoons olive oil,
¼ cup white wine vinegar, 2 teaspoons caster
(superfine) sugar, 2 tablespoons finely chopped
fresh chives and 1 seeded, finely chopped
medium egg (plum) tomato. Cover; refrigerate
30 minutes. Serve zucchini carpaccio sprinkled
with 2 tablespoons roasted slivered almonds.

CARPACCIO

BEEF CARPACCIO

prep time **30 minutes (+ freezing)** serves **8**
nutritional count per serving **7.8g total fat
(2.3g saturated fat); 506kJ (121 cal);
0.3g carbohydrate; 12.3g protein; 0.3g fibre**

Tightly wrap 400g (12½ ounce) piece beef eye
fillet in plastic wrap; freeze 1 hour or until firm.
Unwrap beef; slice as thinly as possible. Arrange
slices on platter. Combine 2 tablespoons olive
oil, 2 teaspoons finely grated lemon rind,
2 tablespoons lemon juice, 1 crushed clove
garlic, ⅓ cup finely chopped fresh flat-leaf
parsley, 2 tablespoons finely chopped fresh
oregano and ⅓ cup finely chopped baby
rocket leaves (arugula) in small bowl. Serve
beef sprinkled with herb mixture and ⅓ cup
flaked parmesan cheese.

KINGFISH CARPACCIO

prep time **30 minutes (+ freezing and refrigeration)**
serves **8** nutritional count per serving **5.7g total fat
(1g saturated fat); 410kJ (98 cal);
0.9g carbohydrate; 10.5g protein; 0.5g fibre**

Tightly wrap 400g (12½ ounce) piece sashimi
kingfish in plastic wrap; freeze 1 hour or until
firm. Unwrap fish; slice as thinly as possible.
Arrange slices on platter; drizzle fish with
¼ cup lemon juice. Cover; refrigerate 1 hour.
Combine 2 tablespoons olive oil, 1 small red
onion, sliced thinly, 1 cup loosely packed fresh
flat-leaf parsley leaves and 2 tablespoons
rinsed, drained baby capers in medium bowl.
Drain juice from fish; serve with onion mixture.
note **Use whatever firm white sashimi-type fish you like.
Raw fish sold as sashimi has to meet stringent guidelines
regarding its handling and treatment after leaving the
water. You should seek local advice from authorities
before eating any raw seafood.**

CHEESE AND SPINACH POLENTA

prep & cook time 45 minutes (+ refrigeration) makes 30
nutritional count per piece 2.6g total fat
(1.3g saturated fat); 242kJ (58 cal);
5.7g carbohydrate; 2.5g protein; 0.5g fibre

1 litre (4 cups) milk
1 cup (170g) polenta
½ cup (50g) coarsely grated mozzarella cheese
¼ cup (20g) finely grated parmesan cheese
250g (8 ounces) frozen spinach, thawed,
    drained, finely chopped
250g (8 ounces) vine-ripened cherry truss
    tomatoes, halved
1 tablespoon balsamic vinegar
1 tablespoon olive oil

1 Grease 20cm x 30cm (8 inch x 12 inch) lamington pan.

2 Bring milk to the boil in medium saucepan; gradually stir in polenta. Cook, stirring, about 10 minutes or until polenta thickens. Stir in cheeses and spinach. Spread polenta mixture into pan, cover; refrigerate 2 hours or overnight or until firm.

3 Preheat oven to 200°C/400°F.

4 Turn polenta onto board; cut into 30 squares. Place polenta onto baking-paper (parchment) lined oven tray. Bake about 20 minutes or until browned lightly.

5 Meanwhile, combine tomato, vinegar and oil in small baking dish. Roast, alongside polenta, about 15 minutes or until tomato softens slightly.

6 Serve polenta squares topped with tomato halves; drizzle with tomato pan juice.

cheese and spinach polenta

marinated mushrooms

MARINATED MUSHROOMS

prep & cook time **40 minutes** makes **4 cups**
nutritional count per ¼ cup **28.6g total fat**
(4g saturated fat); 1145kJ (274 cal);
0.2g carbohydrate; 1.9g protein; 1.3g fibre

1 litre (4 cups) white vinegar
1 cup (250ml) dry white wine
1 tablespoon sea salt flakes
800g (1½ pounds) button mushrooms, halved
2 cloves garlic, sliced thinly
½ teaspoon dried chilli flakes
1 tablespoon coarsely chopped
   fresh rosemary
1 tablespoon finely chopped fresh
   flat-leaf parsley
3 x 5cm (2 inch) strips lemon rind
1 bay leaf
2 cups (500ml) olive oil

1 Sterilise 1-litre (4-cup) jar and lid.
2 Combine vinegar, wine and half the salt
in medium saucepan; heat without boiling.
Add mushrooms; simmer, uncovered, about
5 minutes or until tender. Drain mushrooms;
discard liquid.
3 Combine hot mushrooms, garlic, chilli, herbs,
rind, bay leaf and remaining salt in large
heatproof bowl. Spoon mushroom mixture
into hot sterilised jar.
4 Heat oil in small saucepan; carefully pour
over mushrooms in jar to completely cover
mushrooms, leaving a 1cm (½ inch) space
between mushrooms and top of jar. Seal
while hot.

note To sterilise jars, place cleaned glass jars on their
sides in a large saucepan; cover with cold water. Cover
pan, bring to the boil, and boil for 20 minutes. Carefully
remove jars from water; drain. Stand jars, top-side up,
on a wooden board. The heat from the jars will cause
any remaining water to evaporate quickly. Place jars, on
wooden board, in a cold oven (do not allow the jars to
touch); heat oven temperature to very slow
(120°C/100°C fan-forced), then leave jars in oven for
30 minutes. Plastic screw-top lids give a good seal
(plastic snap-on lids are not airtight enough). Plastic lids
must be well washed, rinsed and dried, or put through
the dishwasher.

fried cauliflower

FRIED CAULIFLOWER

prep & cook time **40 minutes** serves **16**
nutritional count per serving **4.6g total fat**
(1.1g saturated fat); 326kJ (78 cal);
4.9g carbohydrate; 3.7g protein; 1.2g fibre

1 small cauliflower (1kg), cut into florets
3 eggs
½ cup (125ml) milk
½ cup (75g) self-raising flour
¼ cup (20g) finely grated parmesan cheese
2 tablespoons finely chopped fresh
   flat-leaf parsley
vegetable oil, for deep-frying

1 Boil, steam or microwave cauliflower until
tender; drain. Cool.
2 Whisk eggs, milk, flour, cheese and parsley
in medium shallow bowl until smooth.
3 Heat oil in wok. Dip cauliflower into batter;
drain off excess. Deep-fry cauliflower, in batches,
until browned lightly. Drain on absorbent paper.
Serve with lemon wedges.

sweet and sour beetroot

SWEET AND SOUR BEETROOT

prep time **15 minutes** makes **24**
nutritional count per piece **0.8g total fat**
(0.1g saturated fat); 71kJ (17 cal);
1.7g carbohydrate; 0.4g protein; 0.6g fibre

2 large beetroot (beets) (400g), peeled,
    grated coarsely
3 green onions (scallions), sliced thinly
1 tablespoon finely chopped fresh dill
2 tablespoons red wine vinegar
1 tablespoon olive oil
1 teaspoon wholegrain mustard
2 teaspoons caster (superfine) sugar
1 witlof (125g), leaves separated (see note)

1 Combine beetroot, onion, dill, vinegar, oil,
mustard and sugar in medium bowl.
2 Serve beetroot mixture with witlof leaves.
note **You need 24 witlof leaves for this recipe.**

MEATBALLS NAPOLITANA

prep & cook time **1 hour** makes **26**
nutritional count per meatball **3.9g total fat**
(1.2g saturated fat); 305kJ (73 cal);
4.1g carbohydrate; 4.9g protein; 0.8g fibre

500g (1 pound) minced (ground) beef
1 egg
½ cup (50g) packaged breadcrumbs
¼ cup (20g) finely grated parmesan cheese
¼ cup finely chopped fresh flat-leaf parsley
2 tablespoons olive oil
1 small brown onion (80g), chopped finely
1 clove garlic, crushed
700g (1½ pounds) bottled tomato pasta sauce
½ cup (60g) frozen peas
¼ cup coarsely chopped fresh basil

1 Combine mince, egg, breadcrumbs, cheese
and parsley in medium bowl. Using wetted
hands, roll level tablespoons of mince mixture
into balls.
2 Heat half the oil in large frying pan; cook
meatballs, in batches, until browned and
cooked through.
3 Heat remaining oil in same pan; cook onion
and garlic, stirring, until onion softens. Add
sauce; bring to the boil. Add meatballs, reduce
heat; simmer, uncovered, about 10 minutes or
until sauce thickens slightly. Add peas and
basil; simmer, uncovered, until peas are tender.
4 Serve meatballs and sauce with crusty
bread, if you like.

meatballs napolitana

stuffed baby capsicums

STUFFED BABY CAPSICUMS

prep & cook time **1 hour** makes **24**
nutritional count per capsicum **2.6g total fat**
(1g saturated fat); 138kJ (33 cal);
0.5g carbohydrate; 1.9g protein; 0.2g fibre

24 vine sweet minicap baby capsicums
(bell peppers) (350g)
250g (8 ounces) ricotta cheese
2 tablespoons finely grated
parmesan cheese
2 tablespoons coarsely chopped
roasted pine nuts
4 slices hot salami (40g), chopped finely
2 tablespoons finely chopped fresh oregano

1 Preheat oven to 200°C/400°F.
2 Carefully cut tops from capsicums;
reserve tops. Scoop out and discard
seeds and membranes.
3 Combine remaining ingredients in small
bowl. Place mixture in medium piping bag
fitted with 1cm (½ inch) plain tube. Pipe filling
into capsicums; replace tops. Place capsicums,
in single layer, in oiled medium shallow
baking dish.
4 Roast capsicums about 20 minutes or
until tender.

tomato tarts

TOMATO TARTS

prep & cook time **40 minutes** makes **16**
nutritional count per tart **1.2g total fat**
(0.6g saturated fat); 117kJ (28 cal);
3.4g carbohydrate; 0.7g protein; 0.5g fibre

4 medium vine-ripened tomatoes (600g),
peeled, quartered, seeded
1 tablespoon light brown sugar
1 tablespoon balsamic vinegar
½ sheet ready-rolled puff pastry
16 sprigs fresh chervil

1 Preheat oven 220°C/425°F.
2 Combine tomato, sugar and vinegar in
small baking dish; roast, uncovered, about
20 minutes or until tomato is soft.
3 Meanwhile, cut pastry sheet in half lengthways,
cut each half into 4 squares; cut each square
into triangles (you will have 16). Place pastry
triangles on oiled oven tray; top with another
oiled oven tray (this stops the pastry from
puffing up). Bake pastry, alongside tomato,
about 10 minutes or until crisp.
4 Place a tomato piece on each pastry triangle.
Serve topped with chervil.

ARANCINI

prep & cook time **1 hour 30 minutes (+ cooling)**
makes **24** nutritional count per ball **5.7g total fat**
(1.8g saturated fat); 401kJ (96 cal);
8.1g carbohydrate; 1.9g protein; 1g fibre

2 cups (500ml) chicken stock
½ cup (125ml) dry white wine
40g (1½ ounces) butter
1 small brown onion (80g), chopped finely
1 clove garlic, crushed
1 cup (200g) arborio rice
⅓ cup (25g) finely grated parmesan cheese
⅓ cup (35g) coarsely grated
mozzarella cheese
24 fetta-stuffed green olives (240g)
⅓ cup (35g) packaged breadcrumbs
vegetable oil, for deep-frying

1 Combine stock and wine in medium saucepan; bring to the boil. Reduce heat; simmer, covered.

2 Meanwhile, melt butter in medium saucepan; cook onion and garlic, stirring, until onion softens. Add rice; stir over medium heat until rice is coated in butter mixture. Stir in ½ cup of the simmering stock mixture; cook, stirring, over low heat until liquid is absorbed. Continue adding mixture, in ½-cup batches, stirring, until liquid is absorbed after each addition. Total cooking time should be about 35 minutes or until rice is tender. Stir in cheeses, cover; cool 30 minutes.

3 Roll rounded tablespoons of risotto mixture into balls; press an olive into centre of each ball, roll to enclose. Coat risotto balls in breadcrumbs.

4 Heat oil in wok; deep-fry risotto balls, in batches, until browned lightly. Drain on absorbent paper.

arancini

octopus braised with red wine and fennel

OCTOPUS BRAISED WITH RED WINE AND FENNEL

prep & cook time **2 hours** serves **8**
nutritional count per serving **3g total fat**
(0.3g saturated fat); 493kJ (118 cal);
3.1g carbohydrate; 15.2g protein; 1.8g fibre

1 tablespoon olive oil
1 medium brown onion (150g),
   chopped finely
2 cloves garlic, crushed
2 baby fennel bulbs (260g), trimmed,
   chopped coarsely
5 medium vine-ripened tomatoes (560g),
   chopped coarsely
3 bay leaves
1 teaspoon dried chilli flakes
680g (1¼ pounds) whole octopus
⅔ cup (160ml) dry red wine
2 tablespoons finely chopped fresh
   flat-leaf parsley

1 Preheat oven to 200°C/400°F.
2 Heat oil in large frying pan; cook onion and garlic, stirring, until onion softens. Add fennel; cook, stirring, 5 minutes. Add tomato, bay leaves and chilli; cook, stirring occasionally, about 10 minutes or until mixture thickens and fennel is softened.
3 Combine fennel mixture, octopus and wine in medium baking dish; bake, covered, about 45 minutes. Uncover; bake about 40 minutes or until octopus is tender and browned lightly.
4 Cut octopus into bite-sized pieces. Stir in parsley. Serve with crusty bread, if you like.

Soak skewers in water for at least 30 minutes prior to using to prevent them from scorching during cooking.

LEMON, GARLIC AND OREGANO LAMB SKEWERS

prep & cook time **30 minutes (+ refrigeration)** makes **16**
nutritional count per skewer **2.9g total fat**
(1g saturated fat); 284kJ (68 cal);
0g carbohydrate; 10.3g protein; 0g fibre

Cut 800g (1½ pounds) lamb fillets into 2cm (1 inch) pieces. Combine lamb in medium bowl with 1 tablespoon olive oil, 2 teaspoons finely grated lemon rind, 1 clove crushed garlic and 2 tablespoons finely chopped fresh oregano. Cover; refrigerate 1 hour. Stir in 1 tablespoon lemon juice. Thread lamb onto 16 small bamboo skewers or strong toothpicks; cook skewers on heated oiled grill plate (or grill or barbecue) until cooked through.

SUMAC AND SESAME CHICKEN SKEWERS

prep & cook time **30 minutes** makes **16**
nutritional count per skewer **2.6g total fat**
(0.7g saturated fat); 222kJ (53 cal);
0g carbohydrate; 8.1g protein; 0g fibre

Cut 600g (1¼ pounds) chicken breast fillets into 2cm (1 inch) cubes; thread onto 16 small bamboo skewers or strong toothpicks. Combine 1 tablespoon sumac, 1 teaspoon sesame seeds and 1 teaspoon black sesame seeds in small bowl; sprinkle sumac mixture all over skewers. Cook skewers on heated oiled grill plate (or grill or barbecue) until chicken is cooked through. Serve with lemon wedges.

VEGETABLE AND HALOUMI SKEWERS

prep & cook time **35 minutes** makes **16**
nutritional count per skewer **26.2g total fat
(4g saturated fat); 1296kJ (310 cal);
15.6g carbohydrate; 3.4g protein; 0.7g fibre**

Cut 180g (5½ ounces) haloumi cheese into
sixteen 2cm (1 inch) cubes; cut 1 small red
capsicum (bell pepper) into 2cm (1 inch)
pieces. Cut 1 large zucchini in half lengthways;
cut each half into eight 2cm (1 inch) pieces.
Thread haloumi, capsicum and zucchini onto
16 small bamboo skewers or strong toothpicks.
Cook skewers on heated oiled grill plate (or grill
or barbecue) until tender. Meanwhile, combine
½ cup mayonnaise, 1 tablespoon lime juice and
2 teaspoons harissa paste in small bowl. Serve
skewers with lime and harissa mayonnaise.

LAMB KEBABS WITH YOGURT AND PITTA BREAD

prep & cook time **30 minutes** serves **4**
nutritional count per serving **10.8g total fat
(4.8g saturated fat); 1004kJ (240 cal);
5.6g carbohydrate; 29.2g protein; 0.4g fibre**

Combine 500g (1 pound) minced (ground) lamb,
1 egg, 1 finely chopped small brown onion,
2 tablespoons finely chopped fresh flat-leaf
parsley, 1 crushed clove garlic, 2 teaspoons
each ground cinnamon and sweet paprika and
½ teaspoon cayenne pepper in bowl. Form lamb
mixture into 16 sausage shapes, thread onto
16 small bamboo skewers or strong toothpicks;
flatten slightly. Cook on heated oiled grill plate
(or grill or barbecue) until browned and cooked
as desired. Serve kebabs with ½ cup yogurt,
lemon wedges and pita bread.

grilled fetta

GRILLED FETTA

prep & cook time **20 minutes** serves **8**
nutritional count per serving **15.2g total fat**
(5.2g saturated fat); 1150kJ (275 cal);
24.7g carbohydrate; 9.1g protein; 1.6g fibre

200g (6½ ounces) fetta cheese
2 teaspoons olive oil
½ teaspoon sweet paprika
1 loaf ciabatta bread (440g), cut into
  1cm (½ inch) slices
¼ cup (60ml) olive oil, extra
2 teaspoons coarsely chopped fresh
  oregano leaves

1 Preheat grill (broiler).
2 Pat cheese dry with absorbent paper. Place
cheese on oven tray; brush top and sides with
combined oil and paprika. Grill cheese until
browned lightly.
3 Lightly brush both sides of bread with extra
oil. Toast bread on heated oiled grill plate (or
grill or barbecue) until browned both sides.
4 Sprinkle warm cheese with oregano; serve
with toasted bread.
notes Any thick crusty-style bread can be used. Do not
line oven tray with baking paper (parchment) as it may
burn during grilling.

FRIED FISH SANDWICHES

prep & cook time **30 minutes** makes **12**
nutritional count per slice **4.2g total fat**
(1.1g saturated fat); 673kJ (161 cal);
19.5g carbohydrate; 10.1g protein; 1.8g fibre

2 cloves garlic, unpeeled
½ cup (140g) greek-style yogurt
¼ cup finely chopped fresh mint
8 small white fish fillets (320g), skin on
2 tablespoons plain (all-purpose) flour
2 teaspoons smoked paprika
1 teaspoon ground cumin
1 tablespoon olive oil
1 loaf turkish bread (430g), split, toasted
1 baby cos lettuce, leaves separated
2 medium tomatoes (300g), sliced thinly
½ small red onion (50g), sliced thinly

1 Preheat oven to 200°C/400°F.
2 Place garlic on oven tray; roast, uncovered,
about 10 minutes or until soft. Cool; peel garlic.
3 Blend or process garlic and yogurt until
smooth; stir in mint.
4 Coat fish in combined flour and spices;
shake off excess. Heat oil in large frying pan;
cook fish, both sides, until browned and crisp.
5 Spread yogurt over one half of bread; top
with lettuce, tomato, onion, fish and remaining
bread. Cut into 12 slices.
note We used sand whiting fillets in this recipe.

fried fish sandwiches

cheese pastries

CHEESE PASTRIES

prep & cook time **1 hour 15 minutes (+ refrigeration)**
makes **26** nutritional count per pastry **4.7g total fat**
(1.6g saturated fat); 456kJ (109 cal);
12.4g carbohydrate; 4g protein; 0.7g fibre

1½ cups (225g) plain (all-purpose) flour
1½ cups (225g) self-raising flour
½ teaspoon salt
¾ cup (180ml) warm water
¼ cup (60ml) olive oil
1 egg, beaten lightly
2 teaspoons sesame seeds
filling
1 egg, beaten lightly
100g (3 ounces) fetta cheese, crumbled
½ cup (120g) ricotta cheese
½ cup (40g) finely grated romano cheese

1 Preheat oven to 200°C/400°F. Oil oven trays;
line with baking paper (parchment).
2 Process flours and salt until combined. While
motor is operating, add enough of the combined
water and oil so the mixture forms a ball (do
not overmix). Remove dough from bowl, wrap
in plastic; cover, refrigerate 30 minutes.
3 Meanwhile, make filling.
4 Divide dough in half. Roll each half on floured
surface to 30cm x 40cm (12 inch x 16 inch)
rectangle; cut 13 x 8.5cm (3 inch) rounds from
dough. Drop rounded teaspoons of filling onto
rounds; brush edges with a little water. Fold
rounds in half, press edges together with a
fork to seal. Place pastries on trays; brush
with egg, sprinkle with seeds. Bake about
15 minutes or until browned lightly.
filling Combine ingredients in medium bowl.

grilled haloumi

GRILLED HALOUMI

prep & cook time **10 minutes** serves **6**
nutritional count per serving **14.3g total fat**
(9.2g saturated fat); 861kJ (206 cal);
1.7g carbohydrate; 17.8g protein; 0g fibre

500g (1 pound) haloumi cheese
2 tablespoons lemon juice
1 tablespoon coarsely chopped fresh
    flat-leaf parsley

1 Cut cheese into 1cm (½ inch) slices. Cook
cheese on heated oiled flat plate until browned
both sides. Transfer cheese to serving plate;
drizzle with juice. Serve immediately, sprinkled
with parsley.
note **Haloumi is best cooked just before serving as it
becomes tough and rubbery on cooling.**

mini baked herb ricotta

MINI BAKED HERB RICOTTA

prep & cook time **30 minutes** makes **18**
nutritional count per ricotta **1.9g total fat**
(1.1g saturated fat); 105kJ (25 cal);
0.2g carbohydrate; 1.8g protein; 0g fibre

250g (8 ounces) ricotta cheese
1 egg
1 tablespoon finely chopped fresh
   flat-leaf parsley
1 teaspoon finely chopped fresh thyme
1 clove garlic, crushed

1 Preheat oven to 180°C/350°F. Oil 18 holes of two 12-hole (1½-tablespoons/20ml) mini muffin pans.
2 Blend or process ingredients until smooth. Divide mixture among pan holes. Bake about 20 minutes or until browned lightly.

ZUCCHINI FRITTERS WITH SKORDALIA

prep & cook time **1 hour (+ standing)** serves **6**
nutritional count per serving **28g total fat**
(4.2g saturated fat); 1601kJ (383 cal);
26.5g carbohydrate; 5.4g protein; 3g fibre

4 medium zucchini (480g)
2 teaspoons coarse cooking salt
peanut oil, for deep-frying
skordalia
4 slices stale white sandwich bread (180g),
   crusts removed
4 cloves garlic, crushed
½ cup (125ml) olive oil
1 tablespoon lemon juice
1 tablespoon water, approximately
batter
1 cup (150g) self-raising flour
¾ cup (180ml) warm water
1 tablespoon olive oil
1 egg yolk

1 Make skordalia.
2 Cut zucchini into 1cm (½ inch) diagonal slices. Place zucchini in colander, sprinkle with salt; stand 30 minutes. Rinse zucchini under cold water; drain on absorbent paper.
3 Make batter.
4 Heat oil in large saucepan. Dip zucchini into batter, carefully lower into hot oil; cook zucchini until browned and crisp; drain on absorbent paper.
5 Serve zucchini fritters with skordalia.
skordalia Briefly dip bread into a bowl of cold water, then gently squeeze out the water. Blend or process bread and garlic until combined. With motor operating, gradually add oil, juice and enough of the water, in a thin steady stream, until mixture is smooth and thick. Transfer to serving bowl.
batter Sift flour into medium bowl; whisk in combined remaining ingredients until smooth. Stand batter 10 minutes. If batter thickens too much, whisk in a little extra water to give it a coating consistency.

zucchini fritters with skordalia

mini felafel with tomato salsa

MINI FELAFEL WITH TOMATO SALSA

prep & cook time **1 hour 30 minutes (+ refrigeration)**
makes **32** nutritional count per serving **1.4g total fat**
(0.2g saturated fat); 105kJ (25 cal);
2.1g carbohydrate; 0.7g protein; 0.6g fibre

400g (12½ ounces) canned chickpeas
    (garbanzo beans), rinsed, drained
1 small white onion (80g), chopped finely
½ cup finely chopped fresh flat-leaf parsley
2 tablespoons finely chopped fresh
    coriander (cilantro)
2 teaspoons ground cumin
2 teaspoons ground coriander
1 tablespoon finely grated lemon rind
1 teaspoon salt
¼ cup (35g) plain (all-purpose) flour
peanut oil, for deep-frying
tomato salsa
1 medium egg (plum) tomato (75g),
    chopped finely
1 tablespoon coarsely chopped fresh
    coriander (cilantro)
1 tablespoon olive oil

1 To make felafel, blend or process chickpeas, onion, herbs, spices, rind and salt until coarsely chopped. Add flour; process until mixture forms a paste. Transfer mixture to medium bowl; cover, refrigerate 1 hour.
2 Make tomato salsa.
3 Shape felafel mixture between 2 teaspoons into oval shapes. Heat oil in medium deep-frying pan; cook felafel, in batches, until browned. Drain on absorbent paper.
4 Serve felafel with tomato salsa.
tomato salsa Combine ingredients in small bowl.

chilli tomato

ROSEWATER AND SESAME CHICKEN DRUMETTES

prep & cook time **35 minutes (+ refrigeration)** makes **20**
nutritional count per drumette **5.3g total fat**
(1.4g saturated fat); 330kJ (79 cal);
1.3g carbohydrate; 6.8g protein; 0g fibre

20 chicken drumettes (1.4kg)
2 tablespoons light brown sugar
⅓ cup (80ml) rosewater
1 tablespoon olive oil
½ teaspoon ground allspice
2 teaspoons sesame seeds

1 Using small sharp knife pierce chicken all over. Combine chicken, sugar, rosewater, oil and spice in large bowl. Cover; refrigerate 3 hours or overnight.
2 Preheat oven to 220°C/425°F.
3 Place chicken on oiled wire rack over large baking dish; pour over any remaining marinade, sprinkle with seeds. Roast chicken, uncovered, basting with pan juices occasionally, about 30 minutes or until cooked through.

CHILLI TOMATO

prep & cook time **15 minutes** serves **6**
nutritional count per serving **6.2g total fat**
(0.9g saturated fat); 276kJ (66 cal);
1.5g carbohydrate; 0.7g protein; 1.1g fibre

¼ cup coarsely chopped fresh flat-leaf parsley
2 cloves garlic, crushed
½ teaspoon dried chilli flakes
2 tablespoons olive oil
4 large egg (plum) tomatoes (360g),
    sliced thickly

1 Combine parsley, garlic and chilli in small bowl.
2 Heat oil in large frying pan, carefully add tomato in a single layer; cook, over high heat, 2 minutes. Turn tomato, sprinkle with parsley mixture; cook, shaking pan occasionally, about 1 minute or until tomato is caramelised but still holding its shape.
3 Transfer to serving plate; drizzle with pan juices.

rosewater and sesame chicken drumettes

labne

LABNE

prep time **10 minutes (+ refrigeration)** serves **8**
nutritional count per serving **7.2g total fat**
(3.5g saturated fat); 439kJ (105 cal);
6.3g carbohydrate; 3.9g protein; 0g fibre

2 cups (560g) greek-style yogurt
1½ teaspoons fine table salt
1 tablespoon olive oil
½ teaspoon dried chilli flakes
1 tablespoon coarsely chopped
fresh coriander (cilantro)
1 tablespoon coarsely chopped fresh mint

1 Combine yogurt and salt in medium bowl. Place a 12cm (5 inch) diameter strainer over bowl. Rinse cheesecloth in hot water; wring out then line strainer. Place yogurt into strainer; cover with plastic wrap. Refrigerate at least 24 hours to allow to drain.
2 Turn labne onto serving plate, remove cheesecloth; drizzle labne with oil, sprinkle with chilli, coriander and mint.
notes **You need 25cm (10 inch) piece cheesecloth for this recipe; it is available from fabric stores and some kitchenware shops.**
Labne can be drained longer than 24 hours, in fact, 48 hours is better; the longer it is drained the firmer it will become.

lemon pepper squid

LEMON PEPPER SQUID

prep & cook time **30 minutes** serves **4**
nutritional count per serving **8.1g total fat**
(1.7g saturated fat); 953kJ (228 cal);
14.4g carbohydrate; 23.3g protein; 1.7g fibre

500g (1 pound) squid hoods
½ cup (75g) plain (all-purpose) flour
2 tablespoons lemon pepper
2 teaspoons dried rigani or oregano
1 teaspoon coarse cooking salt
peanut oil, for deep-frying
1 tablespoon coarsely chopped fresh parsley

1 Cut squid down centre to open out; score the inside in a diagonal pattern then cut into thick strips.
2 Combine flour, lemon pepper, rigani and salt in large bowl; add squid, toss to coat in mixture, shake away excess.
3 Heat oil in medium saucepan; deep-fry squid, in batches, until tender. Drain on absorbent paper. Serve sprinkled with parsley.
note **Lemon pepper is available from the dried herb and spice section at most supermarkets. If you use one containing salt, reduce the salt quantity in this recipe.**

BASIC PIDE DOUGH

prep & cook time **30 minutes (+ standing)** serves **8**
nutritional count per serving **5.6g total fat**
(0.8g saturated fat); 736kJ (176 cal);
26g carbohydrate; 4.4g protein; 1.6g fibre

Combine 7g (½ ounce) yeast, 1 teaspoon white
sugar, ⅔ cup warm water and 2 tablespoons
warm milk in jug. Stand in warm place until frothy.
Place ½ cup plain (all-purpose) flour in bowl;
whisk in yeast mixture. Cover; stand in warm
place 1 hour. Stir 1½ cups plain flour, 1 teaspoon
salt and 1 tablespoon olive oil into yeast mixture.
Knead dough until smooth. Place in oiled bowl,
cover; stand in warm place 1 hour. Make pide
as per instructions in the following recipes.
For plain pide: preheat oven to 240°C/475°F. Roll
dough into 35cm (14 inch) oval; place on baking
paper (parchment). Make indents with finger
then brush over 1 tablespoon olive oil; sprinkle
with 2 teaspoons black sesame seeds. Heat
oven tray, lift dough onto tray on paper; bake
pide about 15 minutes.

EGG AND CHEESE PIDE

prep & cook time **25 minutes** serves **8**
nutritional count per serving **9.5g total fat**
(2.7g saturated fat); 970kJ (232 cal);
26.3g carbohydrate; 9.3g protein; 1.6g fibre

Preheat oven to 240°C/475°F. Divide 1 quantity
basic pide dough into three pieces; roll each
piece to 12cm x 30cm (5 inches x 12 inches).
Brush edges of dough with a little water; fold
2cm (1 inch) border around edges of dough,
press down firmly. Fold in corners to make oval
shape. Heat oven trays in oven for 3 minutes.
Quickly place pide on hot trays; bake pide
5 minutes. Remove from oven; press centre
of pide down to flatten. Whisk 3 eggs with
90g (3 ounces) coarsely grated haloumi cheese
and 1 finely chopped green onion (scallion) in
large jug. Pour into the cavities of the pide.
Bake further 10 minutes or until set. Cut each
pide into eight slices; serve with lemon wedges.

LAMB AND TOMATO PIDE

prep & cook time **35 minutes** serves **8**
nutritional count per serving **10.5g total fat**
(2.4g saturated fat); 1087kJ (260 cal);
27.5g carbohydrate; 12.6g protein; 2.2g fibre

Preheat oven to 240°C/475°F. Heat 1 tablespoon olive oil in pan; cook 1 chopped brown onion and 1 clove crushed garlic. Add 300g (9½ ounces) minced (ground) lamb, 1 teaspoon each ground cinnamon, cumin and smoked paprika and ½ teaspoon cayenne pepper; cook until lamb is browned. Stir in 1 tablespoon chopped fresh coriander (cilantro); cool. Divide 1 quantity basic dough into three; roll each piece to 12cm x 30cm (5 inches x 12 inches). Spread filling across centre of each piece, leaving 2cm (1 inch) border. Brush edges with water; fold and press around dough. Fold corners to make oval shape. Heat oven trays 3 minutes, place pide on trays; bake 10 minutes. Sprinkle with 1 chopped tomato; bake 5 minutes.

SPINACH AND FETTA PIDE

prep & cook time **25 minutes** serves **8**
nutritional count per serving **10.5g total fat**
(4g saturated fat); 1028kJ (246 cal);
26.5g carbohydrate; 9.9g protein; 2.6g fibre

Preheat oven to 240°C/475°F. Boil, steam or microwave 300g (9½ ounces) spinach until wilted. Rinse, drain then squeeze out excess water; shred spinach finely. Combine spinach, 100g (3 ounces) crumbled fetta cheese and 90g (3 ounces) coarsely grated haloumi cheese in medium bowl. Divide 1 quantity basic dough into three; roll each to 12cm x 30cm (5 inches x 12 inches). Spread filling across centre of each piece, leaving 2cm (1 inch) border. Brush edges with water; fold and press around dough. Fold corners to make oval shape. Heat oven trays 3 minutes, place pide on trays; bake 15 minutes. Cut each pide into eight slices.

TURKISH LAMB FILLO CIGARS

prep & cook time **1 hour 30 minutes** makes **16**
nutritional count per piece **9.4g total fat**
(4.7g saturated fat); 510kJ (122 cal);
4.3g carbohydrate; 5g protein; 0.3g fibre

2 tablespoons olive oil
1 medium brown onion (150g),
   chopped finely
2 cloves garlic, crushed
2 teaspoons each ground allspice and
   ground coriander
1½ teaspoons ground cinnamon
1 teaspoon ground cumin
300g (9½ ounces) lean minced (ground) lamb
1 tablespoon lemon juice
6 sheets fillo pastry
100g (3 ounces) butter, melted
mint yogurt
½ cup (140g) greek-style yogurt
1 tablespoon finely chopped fresh mint

1 Heat oil in medium frying pan, add onion and garlic; cook, stirring, until onion softens. Add spices; cook, stirring, until fragrant. Add mince; cook, stirring until mince is cooked through. Stir in juice; cool.

2 Preheat oven to 220°C/425°F. Oil oven tray; line with baking paper (parchment).

3 Brush 1 sheet of pastry with butter; top with two more sheets, brushing each with butter. Cut layered sheets into 8 rectangles. Press 1 tablespoon of lamb mixture into a log shape along one long end of each rectangle. Roll pastry over filling; fold in sides then roll up to form a cigar shape. Repeat to make a total of 16 cigar shapes.

4 Place cigars, about 2cm (1 inch) apart, on oven tray, brush with remaining butter. Bake about 15 minutes or until browned lightly.

5 Meanwhile, make mint yogurt. Serve warm cigars with mint yogurt.

mint yogurt Combine ingredients in small bowl.

turkish lamb fillo cigars

dolmades

DOLMADES

prep & cook time **3 hours (+ standing)** serves **10**
nutritional count per serving **7.6g total fat**
(1.6g saturated fat); 690kJ (165 cal);
14.9g carbohydrate; 7.7g protein; 3.2g fibre

2 tablespoons olive oil
2 medium brown onions (300g),
    chopped finely
150g (4½ ounces) lean minced (ground) lamb
¾ cup (150g) white long-grain rice
2 tablespoons pine nuts
½ cup finely chopped fresh flat-leaf parsley
2 tablespoons each finely chopped fresh dill
    and finely chopped fresh mint
2 tablespoons lemon juice
1 cup (250ml) water
500g (1 pound) preserved vine leaves
1 cup (250ml) water, extra
1 tablespoon lemon juice, extra
¾ cup (200g) yogurt

1 Heat oil in large saucepan, add onion; cook, stirring, until softened. Add mince; cook, stirring, until mince is browned. Stir in rice and pine nuts. Add herbs, juice and the water. Bring to the boil; reduce heat, simmer, covered, about 10 minutes or until water is absorbed and rice is partially cooked. Cool.

2 Rinse vine leaves in cold water. Drop leaves into a large saucepan of boiling water, in batches, for a few seconds, transfer to colander; rinse under cold water, drain well.

3 Place a vine leaf, smooth side down on bench, trim large stem. Place a heaped teaspoon of rice mixture in centre. Fold stem end and sides over filling; roll up firmly. Line medium heavy-based saucepan with a few vine leaves, place rolls, close together, seam side down on leaves.

4 Pour the extra water over top of rolls; cover rolls with any remaining vine leaves. Place a plate on top of the leaves to keep rolls under the water during cooking. Cover pan tightly, bring to the boil; reduce heat, simmer, over very low heat, 1½ hours. Remove from heat; stand, covered about 2 hours or until all the liquid has been absorbed.

5 Serve with combined extra juice and yogurt.

notes **Use any torn or damaged leaves to line the base of the pan and to cover the rolls. If you don't have enough vine leaves to cover the rolls in the pan, use a circle of baking paper (parchment), then top with the plate. Dolmades are best made a day ahead; store, covered, in the refrigerator.**

veal braciole

4 Thread lemon slices, veal rolls and bay leaves onto 20 small bamboo skewers or strong toothpicks. Brush skewers all over with oil; cook on heated oiled grill plate (or grill or barbecue) until veal is cooked through.

notes We used plain uncrumbed schnitzel, sometimes called escalopes, in this recipe.
You need 20 small bamboo skewers or strong toothpicks for this recipe. Soak skewers in cold water for 30 minutes before using to prevent them scorching during cooking.

GREEK MEATBALLS

prep & cook time **1 hour (+ refrigeration)** makes **50**
nutritional count per meatball **4.7g total fat**
(1.1g saturated fat); 297kJ (71 cal);
2.3g carbohydrate; 4.7g protein; 0.2g fibre

1 tablespoon olive oil
1 medium brown onion (150g), chopped finely
2 cloves garlic, crushed
1kg (2 pounds) lean minced (ground) lamb
1 egg
1½ cups (100g) stale breadcrumbs
2 tablespoons lemon juice
¼ cup finely chopped fresh flat-leaf parsley
¼ cup finely chopped fresh mint
⅓ cup (50g) plain (all-purpose) flour
olive oil, extra, for shallow-frying

1 Heat oil in medium frying pan, add onion and garlic; cook, stirring, until onion is softened. Cool.
2 Combine onion mixture with mince, egg, breadcrumbs, juice, parsley and mint in large bowl. Cover, refrigerate 1 hour.
3 Roll level tablespoons of mixture into balls; toss balls in flour, shake away excess. Heat extra oil in same cleaned pan; shallow-fry meatballs, in batches, until cooked through. Drain on absorbent paper.
4 Serve meatballs with yogurt, if you like.

VEAL BRACIOLE

prep & cook time **40 minutes** makes **20**
nutritional count per piece **1.4g total fat**
(0.2g saturated fat); 184kJ (44 cal);
1.7g carbohydrate; 5.9g protein; 0.3g fibre

⅔ cup (45g) stale breadcrumbs
1 tablespoon rinsed drained baby capers,
    chopped finely
2 cloves garlic, crushed
5 veal schnitzels (500g)
1 medium lemon (140g), quartered,
    sliced thickly
20 fresh bay leaves
1 tablespoon olive oil

1 Combine breadcrumbs, capers and garlic in small bowl.
2 Using meat mallet, gently pound veal, one piece at a time, between sheets of plastic wrap until 5mm (¼ inch) thick; cut each piece in half crossways.
3 Press 1 level tablespoon of crumb mixture over one side of each piece of veal. Roll veal up tightly; cut each roll in half.

greek meatballs

sardines with caper and parsley topping

SARDINES WITH CAPER AND PARSLEY TOPPING

prep & cook time **45 minutes** serves **8**
nutritional count per serving **4.6g total fat**
(0.9g saturated fat); 376kJ (90 cal);
4.8g carbohydrate; 7.1g protein; 0.5g fibre

8 sardines (360g), cleaned
⅓ cup (50g) self-raising flour
½ teaspoon sweet paprika
olive oil, for shallow-frying
caper and parsley topping
2 tablespoons rinsed, drained baby capers,
   chopped finely
1 clove garlic, crushed
¼ cup finely chopped fresh flat-leaf parsley
2 teaspoons finely grated lemon rind
2 teaspoons lemon juice

1 Make caper and parsley topping.
2 To butterfly sardines, cut through the underside
of the fish to the tail. Break backbone at tail;
peel away backbone. Trim sardines.
3 Coat fish in combined flour and paprika;
shake away excess. Heat oil in large frying
pan; shallow-fry fish, in batches, until cooked
through, drain on absorbent paper.
4 Sprinkle fish with caper and parsley topping.
Serve with lemon wedges, if you like.
caper and parsley topping Combine
ingredients in small bowl.

char-grilled banana chillies

CHAR-GRILLED BANANA CHILLIES

prep & cook time **30 minutes** serves **4**
nutritional count per serving **4.8g total fat**
(0.6g saturated fat); 238kJ (57 cal);
2.1g carbohydrate; 0.8g protein; 1.4g fibre

4 red banana chillies (500g)
1 tablespoon white wine vinegar
1 tablespoon olive oil
2 teaspoons finely chopped fresh
   flat-leaf parsley

1 Preheat grill (broiler).
2 Cook whole chillies under hot grill until
blistered and blackened. Cover chillies with
plastic or paper for 5 minutes; peel away skin.
3 Arrange whole chillies on serving plate;
drizzle with combined vinegar, oil and parsley.

OLIVES WITH SAFFRON AND CHEESE

prep time **15 minutes (+ refrigeration)** serves **8**
nutritional count per serving **37.5g total fat**
(9g saturated fat); 1530kJ (366 cal); 0.5g
carbohydrate;7.4 g protein; 1.6g fibre

Combine 1 cup pimiento-stuffed green olives,
1⅓ cups coarsely chopped semi-hard sheep-milk
cheese, 2 thinly sliced garlic cloves, ½ teaspoon
saffron threads and 1 cup olive oil in medium
bowl. Cover, refrigerate overnight or up to
1 week.

note **Sheep-milk cheese can be found in specialty food
stores. It can be substituted with other firm cheeses
such as spanish goat's cheese, provolone or mozzarella.**

MARTINI OLIVES

prep time **15 minutes (+ refrigeration)** serves **8**
nutritional count per serving **17.3g total fat**
(2.5g saturated fat); 711kJ (170 cal);
0.7g carbohydrate; 0.3g protein; 2.9g fibre

Rinse and drain 370g (12 ounces) canned
anchovy-stuffed green manzanilla olives;
combine in medium bowl with 1 tablespoon
finely chopped fresh rosemary, 4 bay leaves,
1 tablespoon extra dry vermouth, 1 tablespoon
gin and ½ cup olive oil. Cover, refrigerate
overnight or up to one week. Serve olives
with crusty bread.

note **Spanish anchovy-stuffed green manzanilla olives
can be found at specialty food stores.**

FENNEL, MINT AND ORANGE OLIVES

prep time **15 minutes (+ refrigeration)** serves **8**
nutritional count per serving **42.9g total fat**
(6.1g saturated fat); 1689kJ (404 cal);
5.2g carbohydrate; 0.4g protein; 0.9g fibre

Combine 1 cup seeded ligurian olives, 1 trimmed,
thinly sliced baby fennel bulb, ½ cup fresh mint
leaves, 2 tablespoons finely grated orange rind,
1 teaspoon black peppercorns and 1½ cups
olive oil in medium bowl. Cover, refrigerate
overnight or up to one week.

note **Ligurian olives are medium-sized black olives
found in specialty food stores; kalamata or any other
black olives can be substituted.**

FIG AND QUINCE PASTE

prep & cook time **3½ hours (+ standing)** makes **4 cups**
nutritional count per teaspoon **0g total fat**
(0g saturated fat); 79kJ (19 cal);
4.5g carbohydrate; 0.1g protein; 0.4g fibre

Peel, core and quarter 1kg (2 pounds) quinces;
combine in large saucepan with 1 cup chopped
dried figs, 1 cinnamon stick and enough water
to cover, bring to the boil. Simmer, covered,
about 1 hour or until most liquid is absorbed.
Discard cinnamon; process mixture until pulpy.
Measure mixture into same pan. Add 1 cup
caster (superfine) sugar to every 1 cup pulp; stir
in ¼ cup lemon juice, stir until sugar dissolves.
Cook, over very low heat, about 2 hours or until
mixture leaves side of pan. Pour into greased
and lined deep 20cm (8 inch) round cake pan.
Stand at room temperature overnight until set.
Serve as part of a cheese platter.

OLIVES & SPREADS

BLUE CHEESE AND CARAMELISED ONION DIP

prep & cook time **30 minutes** makes **1½ cups**
nutritional count per teaspoon **1.7g total fat**
(1.1g saturated fat); 84kJ (20 cal);
 0.7g carbohydrate; 0.4g protein; 0.1g fibre

Melt 20g (¾ ounce) butter in medium saucepan;
cook 1 coarsely chopped large brown onion,
stirring, until onion softens. Add 2 tablespoons
light brown sugar and 2 tablespoons white
wine vinegar; cook, stirring, over low heat,
about 10 minutes or until onion is caramelised.
Stir in 100g (3 ounces) crumbled blue cheese
and ¾ cup crème fraîche until smooth. Cool.
Cover; refrigerate until cold. Stir in ¼ cup finely
chopped fresh flat-leaf parsley.

OLIVES WITH CAPERBERRIES AND SHERRY VINEGAR

prep time **15 minutes (+ refrigeration)** serves **8**
nutritional count per serving **21.6g total fat**
(3.1g saturated fat); 932kJ (223 cal);
7.3g carbohydrate; 0.3g protein; 0.6g fibre

Combine 1¼ cups sicilian green olives, 1 cup
rinsed drained caperberries, 5 sprigs fresh
lemon thyme, ¼ cup sherry vinegar and ¾ cup
olive oil in medium bowl. Cover, refrigerate
overnight or up to 1 week.

PERI PERI OLIVES

prep time **15 minutes (+ refrigeration)** serves **8**
nutritional count per serving **21.6g total fat**
(3.1g saturated fat); 899kJ (215 cal);
5.6g carbohydrate; 0.2g protein; 0.5g fibre

Combine 1¼ cups seeded kalamata olives,
1 tablespoon finely grated lemon rind, 2 halved
fresh small red thai (serrano) chillies, 2 garlic
cloves, ¼ cup red wine vinegar and ¾ cup
olive oil in medium bowl. Cover, refrigerate
overnight or up to 1 week.

BAKED BRIE

prep & cook time **40 minutes** serves **8**
nutritional count per serving **7.3g total fat**
(4.7g saturated fat); 368kJ (88 cal);
0g carbohydrate; 4.8g protein; 0g fibre

Preheat oven to 200°C/400°F. Grease 1 cup
ovenproof dish (10cm diameter, 4cm deep)
(4 inches diameter, 1.5 inches deep.) Place
whole 200g (6½ ounces) brie in dish. Make
six small slits into cheese. Cut 1 sprig fresh
thyme into six pieces; push thyme into slits.
Pour 2 tablespoons dry red wine over cheese;
cover dish, place on oven tray. Bake about
20 minutes. Stand, covered, 5 minutes. Sprinkle
with 1 teaspoon finely grated lemon rind and
1 finely chopped fresh thyme sprig to serve.

ALLSPICE also called pimento or jamaican pepper; a berry, so-named because it tastes like a combination of nutmeg, cumin, clove and cinnamon. Also available ground.

BEANS

broad also known as fava, windsor and horse beans. Fresh and frozen forms should be peeled twice, discarding the outer long green pod and the tough beige-green inner shell.

white in this book, some recipes may simply call for 'white beans', a generic term we use for cannellini, haricot, navy or great northern beans – all of which can be substituted for each other.

CAPERBERRIES fruit formed after the caper buds have flowered; caperberries are pickled, usually with stalks intact.

CAPSICUM also known as bell pepper or, simply, pepper. Comes in many colours: red, green, yellow, orange and purplish-black. Discard seeds and membranes before use.

vine-sweet minicaps can be orange, red or yellow and are about the size of baby red capsicums. Flavoursome with a crispy texture; they have a very fine skin, but still need deseeding.

CAYENNE PEPPER a long, thin-fleshed, extremely hot red chilli usually sold dried and ground.

CHEESE

blue mould-treated cheeses mottled with blue veining. Varieties include firm and crumbly stilton types to mild, creamy brie-like cheeses.

bocconcini baby mozzarella; walnut-sized, delicate, semi-soft, white cheese. Spoils rapidly so must be kept under refrigeration, in brine, for 2 days at most.

cream cheese also known as Philly or Philadelphia, a soft, cows-milk cheese.

fetta a crumbly textured goat or sheep milk cheese with a sharp, salty taste.

goat's made from goat milk; has an earthy, strong taste. Available as soft and firm, and in various shapes and sizes, sometimes rolled in ash or herbs.

haloumi a firm, cream-coloured sheep-milk cheese matured in brine; can be grilled or fried, briefly, without breaking down. Should be eaten while still warm as it becomes tough and rubbery on cooling.

manchego sharp, firm, spanish cheese; found in most specialty food stores. parmesan cheese may be substituted if manchego is not available.

mascarpone a cultured cream product made in much the same way as yogurt. It's a buttery-rich, cream-like cheese made from cows milk. Ivory-coloured, soft and delicate, with the texture of softened butter.

mozzarella a soft, spun-curd cheese. It has a low melting point and wonderfully elastic texture when heated, and is used to add texture rather than flavour.

ricotta the name for this soft, white, cows-milk cheese roughly translates as 'cooked again'. It's made from whey, a by-product of other cheese-making, to which fresh milk and acid are added. Ricotta is a sweet, moist cheese with a slightly grainy texture.

romano a hard cheese with excellent keeping qualities. Made from sheep milk, this straw-coloured cheese has a grainy texture and is mainly used for grating. Substitute with parmesan.

parmesan also known as parmigiano; a hard, grainy, cows-milk cheese. The curd is salted in brine for a month before being aged for up to two years in humid conditions.

CHERVIL also known as cicily; a herb with a mild fennel flavour.

CHILLI available in many types and sizes: generally, the smaller the chilli the hotter it is. Use rubber gloves when seeding and chopping fresh chillies as they can burn your skin. Removing seeds and membranes lessens the heat.

banana also called wax chillies or hungarian peppers; are almost as mild as capsicum but have a distinctively sweet sharpness to their taste. Sold in varying degrees of ripeness, they can be found in pale olive green, yellow and red varieties at greengrocers and most supermarkets.

flakes dried, deep-red, dehydrated chilli slices and whole seeds.

GLOSSARY

long red available both fresh and dried; a generic term used for any moderately hot, long (6cm to 8cm), thin chilli.

thai red also known as 'scuds'; small, very hot and bright red in colour.

CHORIZO a sausage of Spanish origin, made of coarsely ground pork and highly seasoned with garlic and chillies.

COPPA a salted dried sausage made from the neck or shoulder of pork. Is deep red in colour and can be found in both mild and spicy versions.

CORIANDER also known as pak chee, cilantro or chinese parsley; a bright-green leafy herb with a pungent flavour. Stems and roots of coriander may also be used; wash well before chopping. Coriander is also available ground or as seeds, but these are no substitute for fresh coriander as the tastes are very different.

CRÈME FRAÎCHE mature fermented cream having a slightly tangy, nutty flavour and velvety texture. Minimum fat content 35%.

CUMIN also known as zeera or comino.

FENNEL also known as finocchio or anise; a white to very pale green-white, firm, crisp, roundish vegetable about 8-12cm in diameter. The bulb has a slightly sweet, anise flavour but the leaves (fronds) have a much stronger taste. Also the name given to dried seeds having a licorice flavour.

FISH FILLETS, FIRM WHITE any firm white boneless fish fillet – blue eye, bream, swordfish, ling, whiting or sea perch are all good choices. Check for any small pieces of bone in the fillets and use tweezers to remove them.

FLOUR

plain an all-purpose flour made from wheat.

rice a very fine flour made from ground white rice.

self-raising plain flour sifted with baking powder in the proportion of 1 cup flour to 2 teaspoons baking powder.

GHEE also called clarified butter; butter that has had its milk solids removed, so it can be heated to a high temperature without burning.

HARISSA a moroccan sauce or paste made from dried chillies, cumin, garlic, oil and caraway seeds. Is available from Middle-Eastern food stores and major supermarkets.

LEMON PEPPER also called lemon pepper seasoning, a blend of crushed black pepper, lemon, herbs and spices. Is available from the dried herb section at most supermarkets.

MINCE also called ground meat.

OLIVES

anchovy-stuffed green manzanilla medium-sized green or black pickled olives; found at specialty food stores.

fetta-stuffed green green olives stuffed with fetta cheese.

green those harvested before fully ripened and are, as a rule, denser and more bitter than their black relatives.

kalamata small, sharp-tasting, brine-cured black olives.

ligurian very small black olives with a nutty flavour.

niçoise small black olives.

pimiento-stuffed green a green olive with a lively, briny bitterness and stuffed with a morsel of capsicum, which adds a flash of colour.

sicilian dark olive green in colour; can be found almost everywhere olives are sold. Crack but do not seed them, and make certain to alert your guests to the seeds. Brine-cured sicilian olives are smooth and fine-skinned, crisp and crunchy to the bite – they have a refreshingly piquant, buttery flavour.

wild available from select delicatessens. Substitute with small ligurian olives if you can't find them.

PANCETTA pork belly that is cured but not smoked; bacon can be substituted.

PAPRIKA ground dried sweet red capsicum (bell pepper); there are many types available, including sweet, hot, mild and smoked.

POLENTA also known as cornmeal; a flour-like cereal made of dried corn (maize).

POMEGRANATE MOLASSES is thicker, browner and more concentrated in flavour than grenadine, the sweet, red pomegranate syrup used in cocktails. Has a tart, fruity quality similar to balsamic vinegar. It is available from Middle-Eastern food stores, specialty food shops and better delicatessens.

PRAWNS also known as shrimp.

PROSCIUTTO cured, air-dried, pressed ham. Usually sold thinly sliced.

QUAIL small, delicately flavoured, domestically grown game birds ranging in weight from 250g to 300g; also known as partridge.

QUINCE yellow-skinned fruit with a hard texture and an astringent, tart taste; eaten cooked or as a preserve.

RADISH a peppery root vegetable related to the mustard plant. The small round red variety is the mildest.

RAISINS dried sweet grapes.

RIGANI dried a type of oregano but with a stronger flavour; used in many Greek dishes. Available from specialty supermarkets and delicatessens. If unavailable, use dried oregano.

ROCKMELON also known as cantaloupe and musk melon. Has a lovely, moist, sweet orange flesh.

ROSEWATER called gulab in India. An extract made from crushed rose petals; used for its aromatic quality in many sweetmeats and desserts. Available from Middle-Eastern food stores and some delicatessens.

SAFFRON available in strands or ground form; imparts a yellow-orange colour to food once infused. Quality varies greatly; the best is the most expensive spice in the world. Should be stored in the freezer.

SCALLOPS a bivalve mollusc with a fluted shell valve.

SESAME SEEDS black and white are the most common of this small oval seed, however, there are red and brown varieties also.

SOPRESSA a semi-hard pork salami typically flavoured with pepper, cloves, cinnamon, nutmeg, rosemary and garlic. Can be hot or mild.

SPECK also called cured pork.

SUGAR

brown an extremely soft, finely granulated sugar retaining molasses for its characteristic colour and flavour.

caster also known as superfine or finely granulated table sugar.

SUMAC a purple-red, astringent spice ground from berries growing on shrubs that flourish wild around the Mediterranean; adds a tart, lemony flavour to dips and dressings.

VEAL SCHNITZELS a thinly sliced steak available crumbed or plain; we use plain schnitzel, sometimes called escalopes, in our recipes, unless indicated otherwise.

VINE LEAVES from early spring, fresh grapevine leaves can be found in most specialist greengrocers. Alternatively, cryovac-packed leaves in brine can be found in Middle-Eastern food shops and some delicatessens; these must be rinsed well and dried before using. We used vine leaves in brine; available in jars and packets from supermarkets.

VINEGAR

balsamic made from trebbiano grapes; it is a deep rich brown colour with a sweet and sour flavour.

cider (apple cider) made from crushed fermented apples.

red wine based on fermented red wine.

sherry made from a blend of wines and left in wood vats to mature, where they develop a rich mellow flavour.

white made from cane sugar.

white wine made from white wine.

WATERCRESS also known as winter rocket; one of the cress family, a large group of peppery greens. Highly perishable, so must be used as soon as possible after purchase.

WITLOF also known as chicory or belgian endive; its cigar-shaped, tightly packed heads have pale, yellow-green tips, and a delicately bitter flavour. Eaten cooked or raw.

YEAST a 7g (¼ ounce) sachet of dried yeast (2 teaspoons) is equal to 15g (½ ounce) compressed yeast; they can be substituted for each other.

YOGURT we used plain, unflavoured yogurt, unless otherwise specified.

ZUCCHINI also known as courgette; small, pale- or dark-green, yellow or white vegetable belonging to the squash family. Harvested when young, its edible flowers can be stuffed then deep-fried or oven-baked to make a delicious appetiser.

CONVERSION CHART

MEASURES

One Australian metric measuring cup holds approximately 250ml, one Australian metric tablespoon holds 20ml, one Australian metric teaspoon holds 5ml.

The difference between one country's measuring cups and another's is within a 2- or 3-teaspoon variance, and will not affect your cooking results. North America, New Zealand and the United Kingdom use a 15ml tablespoon. All cup and spoon measurements are level. The most accurate way of measuring dry ingredients is to weigh them. When measuring liquids, use a clear glass or plastic jug with metric markings.

We use large eggs with an average weight of 60g.

DRY MEASURES

METRIC	IMPERIAL
15g	½oz
30g	1oz
60g	2oz
90g	3oz
125g	4oz (¼lb)
155g	5oz
185g	6oz
220g	7oz
250g	8oz (½lb)
280g	9oz
315g	10oz
345g	11oz
375g	12oz (¾lb)
410g	13oz
440g	14oz
470g	15oz
500g	16oz (1lb)
750g	24oz (1½lb)
1kg	32oz (2lb)

LIQUID MEASURES

METRIC	IMPERIAL
30ml	1 fluid oz
60ml	2 fluid oz
100ml	3 fluid oz
125ml	4 fluid oz
150ml	5 fluid oz
190ml	6 fluid oz
250ml	8 fluid oz
300ml	10 fluid oz
500ml	16 fluid oz
600ml	20 fluid oz
1000ml (1 litre)	1¾ pints

LENGTH MEASURES

METRIC	IMPERIAL
3mm	⅛in
6mm	¼in
1cm	½in
2cm	¾in
2.5cm	1in
5cm	2in
6cm	2½in
8cm	3in
10cm	4in
13cm	5in
15cm	6in
18cm	7in
20cm	8in
23cm	9in
25cm	10in
28cm	11in
30cm	12in (1ft)

OVEN TEMPERATURES

These oven temperatures are only a guide for conventional ovens.
For fan-forced ovens, check the manufacturer's manual.

	°C (CELSIUS)	°F (FAHRENHEIT)
Very slow	120	250
Slow	150	275-300
Moderately slow	160	325
Moderate	180	350-375
Moderately hot	200	400
Hot	220	425-450
Very hot	240	475

The imperial measurements used in these recipes are approximate only. Measurements for cake pans are approximate only. Using same-shaped cake pans of a similar size should not affect the outcome of your baking. We measure the inside top of the cake pan to determine sizes.

INDEX

If you like this cookbook, you'll love these...